ISBN 1-55912-005-3

© 1995 Anne Geddes 1995

Published in 1995 by Cedco Publishing Company,
2955 Kerner Blvd, San Rafael, CA 94901.
First USA edition 1995.

ANNE GEDDES ™
is the registered trademark
of The Especially Kids Company Limited.

Designed by Jane Seabrook
Produced by Kel Geddes
Colour separations by HQ Imaging
Typesetting by Advision
Printed through Colorcraft, Hong Kong

A

ANNE GEDDES

A

Angel

B

Bee

C

Cat

D

Duck

E

Egg

F

Fairy

G

Grandpa

H

Hat

I

Inside

J

Jack-in-a-box

K

Kiss

L

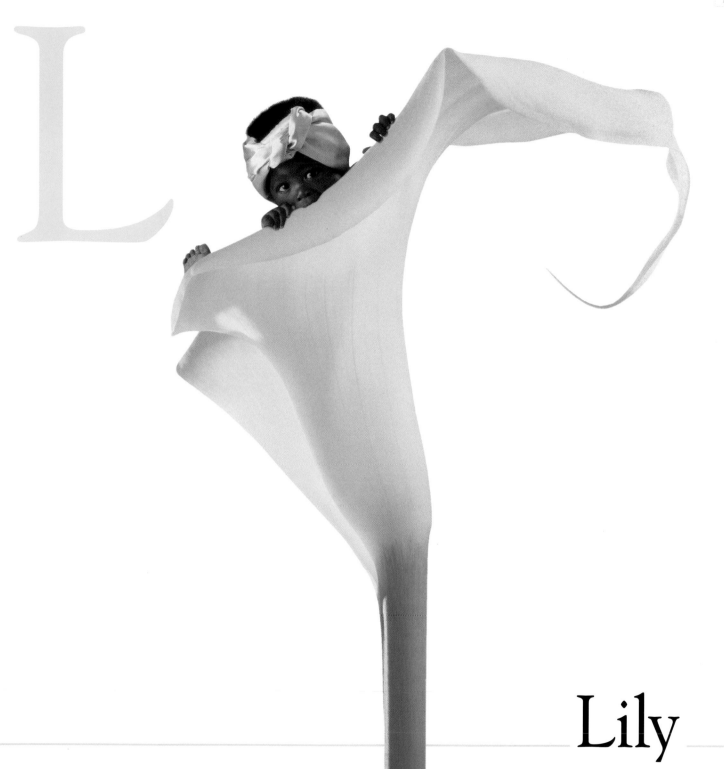

Lily

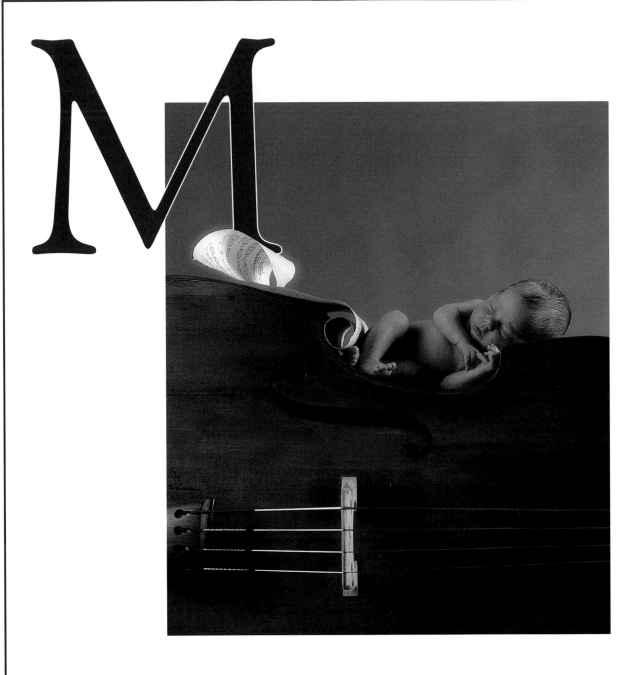

M

Music

N

Nest

Oh no!

P

Pumpkin

Queen

R

Rose

S

Sunflower

T

Tulip

U

Upside-down

V

Valentine

W

Washtub

X

Merry Xmas

Xmas short for Christmas

Y

Yawn

Z

Zzzzz